# My Testimony: Positive Thoughts and Affirmations

By
Hollye Murray Nicholas

Copyright © 2024

All Rights Reserved

ISBN:

978-1-963502-44-2 (Paperback)

# Table of Contents

About the Author ................................................................... 3
Introduction ........................................................................... 4
Long Thoughts: Life Is Supposed to Be a Struggle ............ 1
Live Your Life While You Have It ....................................... 2
We Can Be Happy Because God Has a Plan ....................... 3
Our Obligation to Be Missionaries ....................................... 4
We Cannot Be Christians Without God's Help ................... 6
The Game of Life .................................................................. 9
Do Your Best to Guard Your Money .................................. 10
Friends .................................................................................. 11
Short Thoughts .................................................................... 12
You Have to Learn Hard to Do Easy ................................. 16
Minimize the Negative ........................................................ 17
Positive Affirmations .......................................................... 27
Thoughts on Death .............................................................. 36
Death Is a Passage Way to Heaven .................................... 38
Everything Will Be Okay ................................................... 41
A Big Part of Life Is Coping with Death .......................... 42
Bible Verses ........................................................................ 45

# About the Author

Hollye Murray Nicholas is a retired teacher from New Orleans, Louisiana, who now lives with her husband and son in Baton Rouge, Louisiana.

# Introduction

I did not intend to write a book. After praying, I would get thoughts and write them. After a while, I had many thoughts that I would share with family and friends. They said the thoughts were good and I should write a book. I started to believe that my thoughts could help others, so I decided to write this book. These are my Christian beliefs. I do not intend to offend believers of other religions. I respect other religions and the right of people to choose whatever beliefs they choose to practice. These are only *my* beliefs. Anyone can disagree with me. So many family members and friends encouraged me. Unfortunately, I cannot name them all. I simply request that they forgive me if their names are not mentioned in this book.

I must acknowledge my son, Andres P. Nicholas Jr., who was my inspiration and editor. My husband, Andres P. Nicholas Sr., for greatly encouraging me throughout the process. Allison Story and Elaine Wolo also helped me. Roslyn Terrell supported me along the way.

Allison introduced me to her cousin, Jamal Story, a great and talented dancer, entertainer, and author, who graciously walked me through this process. I am eternally grateful to all of the people who supported me. I sincerely hope this book can lead others to become Born-Again Christians by knowing God through our Savior Jesus Christ. Anyone who wants to be a Born-Again believer, please pray the following prayer:

"Dear Lord, please make me Born-Again. I now accept Jesus as my personal Savior, and I believe that He died for all of my sins. Please save me and help me to believe that I am saved. Please help me to give up my sins. In Jesus's name. Amen."

Anyone who is interested in spreading the Gospel and

encouraging others to become Born-Again, please consider passing out the religious papers, which are located at the back of this book. It is my sincere hope that the reader of this book can enjoy peace while going through the many challenges of life. May God bless all of you.

# Long Thoughts: Life Is Supposed to Be a Struggle

Because life is supposed to be a struggle, we must have faith in God to help us succeed during our journey of life. If we expect life to be easy, we set ourselves up for heartache and defeat. The only way we can win at the game of life is to be Born-Again believers who relinquish total and complete control of our lives to God. In spite of all of the problems in life we can have peace because **Isiah 26:3** says, *"You will keep in perfect peace all who trust in you, whose thoughts are fixed on you."* In **John 16:33**, Jesus said, *"These things I have spoken to you, that in Me you may have peace."* In the world you will have tribulation; but be of good cheer, I have overcome the world."

God and Jesus have seen Heaven, and they know the future of our lives. However, we have never seen Heaven and do not know the future. That is why we have to have faith. Sometimes, it is difficult to have faith, but we should pray for it and believe we have it. If we say and affirm that we have it, then we will obtain it over time. **Psalm 50:15** says, *"Trust in Me in your times of trouble and I will rescue you and you will give Me glory."*

So, expect trouble but also expect peace and know that you will be rescued and God will solve all your problems if you are a Born-Again believer who trusts in Him and keeps the faith.

# Live Your Life While You Have It

Enjoy your life while alive without predicting when your life will end. This will enable you to live your best possible life. What you put in your mind could possibly have a lot to do with your health. If you think gloomy thoughts, your body may adapt to that way of thinking, and you might develop physical problems. Confidence is a game-changer. Having confidence and perseverance will determine whether or not a person is successful. If you go into a ball game with negative thoughts, your chances of losing that game increase.

# We Can Be Happy Because God Has a Plan

We can be happy despite living in this world where we see many adverse events because we know God is in control. He will make everything right in the end.

**Roman 8:28** says, *"And we know that in all things God works for the good of those who love him, who have been called according to his purpose."* It is a privilege and honor to do God's work. Even though many of us look forward to being in Heaven with God and Jesus, we do not have to rush away from our earthly lives because peace is available to the children of God on Earth. He holds the hands of His Born-Again children throughout their journey of life.

*HOLLYE MURRAY NICHOLAS*

# Our Obligation to Be Missionaries

As Born-Again Christians, it is our obligation because of the great commission, as stated in the Bible, to tell others about becoming Born-Again. Someone becomes Born-again by accepting Jesus Christ as their personal Savior and saying the following prayer:

"Dear Lord, please make me Born-Again. I am now accepting Jesus as my personal Savior, and I believe that He died for all of my sins and that You raised Him from the dead. Please save me and help me to believe that I am saved. Also, please help me give up my sins and live a Christian life. In Jesus's name. Amen."

As Born-Again Christians, it is our obligation to spread the Gospel of following Jesus to become Born-Again. This obligation is revealed by the great commission as stated in the Bible where Jesus said in **Matthew 28:19-20**, *"Therefore go and make disciples of all nations, baptizing them in the name of the Father and of the Son and of the Holy Spirit, and teaching them to obey everything I have commanded you. And surely, I am with you always, to the very end of the age."* We can easily accomplish this mission by passing out religious tracts or papers (there is one printed on the back of this book, which you can consider copying and passing out without putting pressure on anyone). You do not have to say much. Not everyone has a gift of speech regarding religious matters. However, if you do have that gift, please consider telling others about becoming Born-Again in a non-judgmental way at the appropriate time and place. Always be respectful (and careful) and do this in a way that is safe for you and others.

*HOLLYE MURRAY NICHOLAS*

# We Cannot Be Christians Without God's Help

Do not feel that you have to be perfect to live a Christian life. It is a constant struggle. God is always encouraging His Born-Again children because life is hard. **Psalms 34:19** says, *"The righteous person may have many troubles, but the Lord delivers him from them all."* **Philippians 4:6-7** says, *"Do not be anxious about anything, but in every situation, by prayer and petition, with thanksgiving, present your request to God and the peace of God which transcends all understanding will guard your hearts and your minds in Christ Jesus."* **Psalms 50:15** says, *"And call on me in the day of trouble, I will deliver you and you will honor me."*

Many Christians constantly struggle with fear and must depend on the Lord to make it. They do not have it together all the time. **Isaiah 41:10** says, *"So do not fear for I am with you, do not be dismayed, for I am your God. I will strengthen you and help you. I will uphold you with my righteous right hand."* Many Born-Again Christians still have conflict between good and evil and must put on the armor of God to defeat Satan, as explained in **Ephesians 6:11**. For example, if someone does you wrong, most people have trouble forgiving and loving that person. Sometimes, the Devil is more after true Christians than the sinners. Christians also have temptations.

However, they depend on God to help them overcome temptations. **1 Corinthians 10:13** says, *"No temptation has overtaken you except what is common to mankind. And God is faithful; He will not let you be tempted beyond what you can bear. But when you are tempted, He will also provide a way out* *so that you can endure it."* As stated in **1 Peter 5:8-10**, *"Stay alert! Watch out for your great enemy, the Devil. He prowls around like a roaring lion, looking for someone to devour. Stand firm against him, and be strong in your faith. Remember that your family of believers all over the world is going through the same kind of suffering you are. In His kindness, God called you to share in His eternal glory by means of Christ Jesus. So, after you have suffered a little while, He will restore, support, and strengthen you, and He will place you on a firm foundation."*

Sometimes, Christians have to pour out their hearts to God. He hears and helps them. God is available to help every one of His Godly children. **Psalms 34:17** says, *"The righteous cry out and the Lord hears them. He delivers them from all their trouble."* Likewise, **2 Peter 2:9** says, *"If this is so, then the Lord knows how to rescue the Godly from trials and to hold the unrighteous for punishment on the day of judgment."*

Everyone can have all of the blessings of a Christian by asking for forgiveness and by praying this prayer:

"Dear Lord, please make me Born-again. I am now accepting Jesus as my personal Savior, and I believe that He died for all of my sins and that You raised Him from the dead. Please save me and help me to believe that I am saved. Please help me to give up my sins. In Jesus's name. Amen."

**Isaiah 48:22** says, *"There is no peace,"* says the LORD, *"for the wicked."* **Psalms 29:11** says, *"The Lord gives strength to His people; the Lord blesses His people with peace."* The needs of the true Christian will be met by God. **Matthew 6:31-33** says, *"So don't worry about these things, saying, 'What will we eat? What will we drink? What will we wear?' These things dominate the thoughts of unbelievers, but your Heavenly Father already knows all your needs. Seek the Kingdom of God above all else, and live righteously, and He will give you everything."*

**Malachi 3:10** says, *"Bring the whole tithe into the storehouse, that there may be food in my house. Test me in this,"* says the Lord Almighty, *"and see if I will not throw open the floodgates of heaven and pour out so much blessing that there will not be room enough to store it."* The Lord gives Godly people their God-given wants. **Psalms 37:4** says, *"Delight yourself in the Lord, and He will give you the desires of your heart."* Most of all, God does not want us to give up and stop believing in Him. **Galatians 6:9** states, *"Let us not become weary in doing good, for at the proper time we will reap a harvest if we do not give up."*

Christians are human, and there are times when they question God. However, they must pray to Him to help them believe and keep their faith. **Romans 8:28** says, *"And we know that in all things God works for the good of those who love Him, who have been called according to His purpose."* Born-again Christians are former sinners who have been saved by His Grace, a gift from God. Doing good work does not save anyone.

# The Game of Life

Life is like a football game because the offense is trying to get a touchdown. The football player running with the ball is like a dreamer who has a dream. The offensive line helps the runner get a touchdown, just like the friends of the dreamers help them reach their goals. The defensive line is trying to stop the player with the ball from making a touchdown, just like many envious people try to prevent dreamers from obtaining their objectives. However, the dreamers need to keep going, press on, and never give up because the ones who keep striving are the ones who obtain their goals.

# Do Your Best to Guard Your Money

It is possible that some people will take your possessions. It is just a fact of life, no matter how careful you are. Therefore, you should buy what you really want within reason and enjoy it. Do not spend all your money and live above your means, but if you see something you really want and can afford, you should get it. You deserve it more than anyone else. Do not get into trouble, but do your best to stop people from wrongfully taking things that belong to you. However, if you cannot lawfully stop them without jeopardizing your safety, put it in God's hands and do not worry. God will make things right in the end for His children.

# Friends

There are three types of friends: false friends, temporary friends, and true friends. Sometimes, you cannot tell the difference between the three.

The false friends were never your friends in the first place. Temporary friends are your friends for a short time, and they turn against you for an unknown reason even though you have not done anything wrong. It is better to let them go, love them in Christian love from a distance, and forgive them. Then there are true friends who are your friends for life. It has been said that true friends are precious and rare, but false friends are everywhere. If there is a disagreement with someone you think is a true friend, it is worth trying to solve the problem and keep the friend. We do not always know who our true friends are, so it is good to be kind to everyone. Sometimes, the person you think is your true friend can disappoint you during your most desperate time of need. The person who may seem irrelevant may be a sincere friend who comes to your rescue during a crucial time. Treat everyone with the same respect regardless of their position in life.

Everyone is important. It would be wonderful if we could all strive to be true, lifelong friends to our friends.

# Short Thoughts

Do not let anyone who treats you unfairly mess up your day. Do not give them that power and satisfaction. They will do wrong to anyone who is in your position. Respond to them in a Godly calm way, and enjoy the rest of your day. This will please God and frustrate the person who is controlled by Satan.

Do not try and fight the devil on your own because he is the master of evil. If you do, God will not help you and you will lose because the devil is very powerful. In order to get God's help, you must put on the full armor of God as stated in Ephesians 6:10. In this way you will not only win the battle, but you will automatically win the entire war.

The life of the believer is like a perfectly constructed puzzle. Periodically, there may be rough times, but in the end, *"God works for the good of those who love him, who have been called according to his purpose,"* as stated in **Romans 8:28** (NIV).

In the end, the life of a believer works together like the ingredients of a fine entree.

Worrying will not change circumstances. It could only bring distress and possible illness. The best you can do is to be sure that you are Born-Again. You should also pray, have faith, trust God, and follow His guidance.

Sometimes, looking to others to love us is discouraging and disappointing. We should mainly look to God and Jesus because they accept and love us no matter what we do. Their love is enduring. God forgives us no matter what if we are born again and if we repent.

Do not let anxiety stop you from starting anything. The only way you can finish is if you start. A big part of life is coping with multiple problems. Climb every mountain one step at a time.

Do not worry about things changing or good items being discontinued. God will fix it by providing a substitute or working things out so you do not need the missing item.

For the Born-Again Christian, their body is like a capsule, whose important part is what is on the inside. The capsule is transferred when the soul goes to Heaven.


Many have said that practice makes perfect. However, you have to practice correctly so that you are not perfectly wrong.


If you are Born-Again, no matter what comes, it is better to face it with God than to face it alone. He will make everything right in the end. Your enemies are in front of you, and they are small. God, Jesus, and the Holy Spirit are behind you and on your side. They are big, all-powerful, and all-knowing. Because of that, you will win the battle and ultimately win the war.


You have the victory in all things. With God's help, you are a conqueror and an overcomer.


If you are Born-Again, you should pray, believe, and do your best; God will do the rest. You can count on Him to make things right in the end.


You cannot have everything you want, so enjoy what you

have because God gives you everything you need.

# You Have to Learn Hard to Do Easy

Do not be so busy trying to stay alive that you do not enjoy being alive. Do your best to care for yourself and protect your life, but ultimately depend on God. Pray for and follow God's guidance regarding your personal safety and protection, but do not be so fearful of protecting that you forget to enjoy your life.

Whenever you gain something, you also gain its problems. It is not a good idea to force something. If it is God's will for you to have it, He will solve the problems that you encounter.

Do not focus on your problems and forget your blessings. Instead, you should focus on your blessings and minimize your problems.

Take the positive and spread it as far as it can go.

# Minimize the Negative

Hold dear your loved ones who are still here with you. Tell them that you love them often. Cherish every moment that you have with them.

Do not regret your mistakes. Everything is a learning experience. Embrace the lesson, learn from it, move on, and do better.

Do not wait until a certain event occurs to be happy. That event may never happen, or something negative may occur. You already know what is happening now, so be happy. Look at all the positive things presently occurring in your life and be happy.

No matter how late in life that God guides your thoughts, just be grateful.

Do not be in awe or surprised over the magnitude of evil things that evil people do. They are controlled by Satan. Just keep depending and believing in God.

Today is automatically a good day because God made it and allowed me to see it. Every day is a blessing.

Jesus is the only true representative of God. Do not turn against God because of what some people do.

Think about all the blessings that you waited for and received. Enjoy those blessings.

No matter what you do and how much you beg, God's will is going to prevail. The only way we can know His will is to pray about and attempt to do lawful things we would like to happen.

Do not rush and make a quick decision that you will regret later. It is better not to do anything than to do the wrong thing. Your mistake can put you in a worse situation than the initial problem you were trying to solve.

Some of the many ways that God speaks to us are by putting ideas in our minds while we are awake, through dreams, by telling others who give us the message, and by any other way that He deems necessary.

If someone loves the Lord, we do not have to worry about them because they will be all right. God will take good care of them. **Romans 8:28** says, *"And we know that God works all things together for the good of those who love Him, who are called according to His purpose."* If they are not Born-Again, we should pray that they become Born-Again.

You will always be hated by somebody. Let them hate you because you are doing good things and not because you are doing bad things. Be good and stand with Jesus because you will be in good company.

Do not worry about yesterday and what I did not do. Be glad for today and what I am doing. Also, be glad for tomorrow and what I will do.

When a puzzle piece is taken from our lives because of a wrong done to us, God replaces that puzzle piece by compensating us. We should not anxiously wait to receive our compensation. It is better to enjoy our lives and loved ones now.

Life is like a roller-coaster. They both have ups and downs, but we should not worry because **Psalm 46:1-2** says, *"God is our refuge and strength, an ever-present help in trouble. Therefore, we will not fear, though the earth give way and the mountains fall into the heart of the sea."* God's help will comfort us and get us through the difficult situation.

We should not fight Satan alone after he antagonizes us because we will always lose. We should fight him by using the armor of God, as stated in **Ephesians 6:10-18** so that God will help us defeat Satan.

The longer I live, the more I realize how little I know compared to how much God knows.

Do not rush through things that take a long time. Take your time and do a good job.

Not every battle is worth fighting, so carefully choose which one you will deal with.

Do not be so distracted with battles that you let important things go undone. **Ecclesiastes 3:1** says, *"There is a time for everything, and a season for every activity under the heavens."*

The evil people reign for a while and accomplish many evil things, but God's people will prevail in the end.

Evil people are smart, manipulative, and controlling. They can influence many. However, when God's people pray and ask Him for wisdom and discernment, they can recognize the conniving ways of the wicked.

Do not let the misery of your enemy become your misery. Many miserable people hurt others. God is punishing them for the wrong that they have done to you. However, we should not delight in their punishment. Despite the wrong you have endured, peace is available to all Born-Again believers who ask for it and believe that God will give it to them. **Psalm 29:11** says, *"The Lord gives strength to His people; the Lord blesses His people with peace."*

Sometimes, there is confusion because we misunderstand people and misread their motives. There is no confusion regarding God. We know that He is with us. **Romans 8:28** says, *"And we know that in all things God works for the good of those who love Him, who have been called according to His purpose."*

To appreciate easy times, you must have gone through the hard times. Many people who have always had it easy do not appreciate it. They collect things the same way that people collect charms on a bracelet.

Pray for your enemy's salvation, and move on with your life.

Do not think about how the Devil is working in evil people. Instead, think about how God is working in you. Change your perspective and focus on positive things. With God's help, have peace and joy despite it all.

Everyone has past baggage. Ask God to help you to forget it and to forgive yourself. Enjoy and cherish the good things that are presently happening in your life.

No matter what happens in the world, God's plan for our lives will prevail.

The only good kind of revenge that you can have against an enemy is to be happy and forgive them so that they do not stop you from receiving eternal life. Let God deal with them.

When you see someone with exceptional talent, do not idolize them. Instead, praise God because He gave them that talent.

Satan is our only enemy. He works through different people and in some of our thoughts. We should give our problems to God and receive His peace and happiness.

Clear out the weeds and start anew. Keep watering your dreams. You may be in for a pleasant surprise.

Do your best, and God will handle the rest.

To have peace, a believer must pray and look at the world through the glasses of faith and positivity.

Use wisdom gained from past mistakes to make wise choices in the present and the future.

Yesterday's future is today. Stop living for the future and enjoy today.

If we wait until everything is good, we will never be happy. There is always something good happening. Often, good things are right before our eyes, but we do not recognize them because we dwell on the bad. We should pray that we can recognize and focus on the good and receive God's peace.

God's power keeps us spiritually charged with faith and peace.

Anything that involves man is never one hundred percent

good or bad. Only God, Jesus, and the Holy Spirit are good.


My peace is more important than the punishment of my enemies.


God knows who loves Him and who is saved. He knows what a dead person would have done if they had lived. God gives everyone a chance to be saved. This is not for us to worry about. We should spread the Gospel to as many people as possible and pray they will go to Jesus and be Born-Again. We should pray for everyone to be saved. If we have spread the Gospel to someone who later dies, we would have peace knowing that we have done our best to help them get in touch with the only one who can save them – Jesus Christ.


Just like a house does not build itself, the world did not build itself. It needed a creator.


Do not hate anyone. Do not let children of the dark cause us to become a child of the dark. Even if we feel justified to hate them because they have done us wrong, continue to love and forgive them so that we can be children of the light.

The best revenge is to love them and forgive them so that they do not stop us from receiving eternal life.

It is better to forgive your enemies even if you have to beg God to help you to forgive them. They may do just enough to get eternal life at the last minute. It would be a tragedy for you to miss out on eternal life because of something that they did to you. Being a victim in the first place is wrong, but it would be an even greater wrong to let them stop you from living forever. Pray to God for help if you must, but please find a way to forgive them and move on.

# Positive Affirmations

Today is a good day because God is in charge, and He is causing me to deal with everything successfully. I am enjoying each moment.

God is a better friend to me than anybody else. He is a better friend to me than I am to myself. I will talk to God, confide in Him, and trust Him. He comforts my soul and gives me the strength to live with confidence.

With God's help, I am strong, and I am brave. Nothing will defeat me. He is taking care of me, and all is well.

God's plan is better than my plan. He is in control. God is not limited by any rules, and He can do what He wants to do. Everything that God does is for our benefit. **1 Thessalonians 5:16-18** says, *"Be joyful always; pray continually; give thanks in all circumstances, for this is God's will for you in Christ Jesus."* I have joy because I know God is taking good care of me.

God is a Miracle worker. I will not try to figure out everything.

I will just trust Him.

God's will is always best for me, even if it brings hardship. The end result is always good. It may take a while before I can see the good, but I will continue to have faith in Him.

With God's help, I have peace during challenging times. No matter what happens, today is a good day because God is fixing everything for my good. He is making all things right in His time and in His way.

God loves me. He has my best interest at heart. He is doing what is best for me. I will not worry.

With God's help, I will not let my enemies disgust or anger me. I will look at life through the eyes of peace.

I am not just anybody. I am a child of God with special help and protection from Him.

With God's help, I am calm and strong. God is with me all of the time. Everything is and will be all right.

God is my Father, and He is in charge forever. Jesus will always be my Savior. Because of this, I am exceedingly happy and have no reason to worry.

There is a blessing somewhere in this trouble, and I will see it one day. God will adequately compensate me. Because of that, I can have peace in spite of it all.

God is enabling me to handle every situation successfully. Because of that, I am enjoying every day. I do not fear anything because I know God is with me and that He is helping me.

God is strengthening me and enabling me to cope with all things. **Romans 8:28** says, "*And we know that God works all things together for the good of those who love Him, who are called according to His purpose.*"

Even though I am in the midst of troubling times, I will remember that God loves me and that He will solve all of my problems.

With God's help, I have the victory. I am thinking, saying, and doing the right things.

I have no fear because I have faith in God. He is leading me, and I am following His guidance.

With God's help, I have great abilities that I will use to accomplish great things.

I am able to handle everything. I am indestructible because God has given me special skills that enable me to successfully handle life as long as I believe and depend on Him.

God is helping me with everything. With His help, I am happy, and I have peace forever.

Even though I have gut-wrenching problems, I will still be

happy. God has made peace available for every Born-Again believer. He has promised to give us peace if we meet the conditions of **Isaiah 26:3**, which says, *"You will keep in perfect peace all who trust in you, all whose thoughts are fixed on you!"* With God's help, I will meet His conditions and receive His peace.

God holds my hand as I walk through the journey of life. I know that the end is good. I am living in peace, joy, and happiness for the rest of my life.

In spite of the trouble on Earth, I will make it with God's help.

The Lord is helping me to get crucial things done in a timely way without being overwhelmed. Because of Him, I will not get frustrated. He is helping me rearrange my schedule and to adapt to change.

I do not want to worry about anything. With God's help, I will not worry. I am praying for peace, and with His help, I will have it.

I am not struggling. I am overcoming problems. With God's

help, I am smart and good. He protects me from evil. He is leading and guiding me. I will recognize and follow His guidance. I am special because I am God's child.

The Bible says, "I can do everything through Christ who strengthens me." Because of Him, I am indestructible.

I trust God, and I have peace, happiness, and strength. Because of Him, my concentration is good. He is leading me, and I am following His guidance.

I am enjoying my blessings. God is giving me all my needs for the rest of my life. **Luke 12:31** states, *"He will always give you all you need from day to day if you will make the Kingdom of God your primary concern."*

I am enjoying all of the good things in my life. I am forgiving all of my enemies because God is with me. I do not fear anything.

I love God. He is encircling me with His love and strength.

I am grateful to God for the wisdom I have attained from bad experiences that have made me better.

I totally believe in God. I am not worried about anything. God is cleansing my soul, and He is making me whole. God is supreme. He is giving me everything I need.

God is controlling my thoughts, speech, and actions. He is the Creator of the Universe. God is all-powerful, all-knowing, and omnipresent. He makes a way in a situation that is humanly impossible to solve.

God is helping me to let go of past regrets because of Him. I am not anxious about the future. He is helping me to enjoy the present and to live with the expectancy of great things.

Because of the Lord, I am happy, and I have peace. The Lord is solving all of my problems and controlling me in every way. God is causing me to deal with all situations victoriously. Because of that, I will have sufficient faith and not worry.

The Lord is helping me to accept His will. He is protecting me from the Devil.

More than being someone's child, someone's spouse, and someone's parent, I am God's child. God loves me forever, no matter what. Because of that, I have a reason to be happy. He will never change. I can always depend on Him. I am grateful to God for the good things He has given me. I am glad He makes everything good in the end,

in His time and in His way.

God Almighty is in charge, and right will prevail.

God is helping me to handle stress and not be overwhelmed. I am getting crucial things done on time. He is helping me with everything.

I will not be anxious and rush to get things done. I will look around me and realize that it took many years to do the things that I have already done. I will enjoy and appreciate what I have already accomplished. I will pace myself and not be anxious to do the things I must do in the future.


    I am content with what the Lord has given to me. I will pray and believe that He will meet all of my needs. **Philippians 4:19** says, *"And my God will supply all of you needs according to His riches in glory in Christ Jesus"*. God has arranged everything to work out in my favor. **Romans 8:28** says, *"And we know that in all things God works for the good of those who love Him, who have been called according to His purpose."* I believe that everything will be all right.

# Thoughts on Death

For the Born-Again Christian, death is like a promotion on a job or graduation from school, where the dead leave the old life and go to the Holy afterlife.

We are only on the earth with our family and friends for a little while. Therefore, we should love each other and treat each other right while we are here so that we will have a clear conscience if anything bad happens. We should cherish our time together and tell them we love them.

Our deceased loved ones belong to and are focused on a different world. We must let them go and let God care for them without worrying. When events happen on earth, we should share them with our living loved ones. We should be grateful that we still have their company. As always, our main concentration should be on God.

We ought to cherish and treasure our memories of our deceased loved ones, but we should also enjoy the present.

A deceased Christian's death day is their birthday in Heaven. It is probably the best day of their lives. There will be a celebration in Heaven when they arrive.

*HOLLYE MURRAY NICHOLAS*

# Death Is a Passage Way to Heaven

Do not think about where your Born-Again deceased loved one was, but think about where they are now. Do not think about what they left behind; instead, think about where they went. They went to a wonderful and beautiful paradise. Nothing can be better than that. They are dead in this world but alive in Heaven, and we should have peace in this situation.

Do not live in fear of the death of your loved ones or yourself. We should live each day and try to be happy.

Death is just a passageway to eternal life.

How can God cause people to die when we want to live? It is because God knows what a beautiful place the next world is for Born-Again Christians. We can only believe great things about paradise, but God actually knows about it.

Jesus had to die, and so do we. Death is just a change of

address. They have moved to another home. The Born-Again deceased Christians are still alive. They are more than just a memory. The Bible says in **John 3:16**, *"For God so loved the world that He gave his one and only Son, that whoever believes in Him shall not perish but have eternal life."*

Since they are so happy, why are we so sad? We should rejoice in knowing that they are saved, they know God, and that they are with God and Jesus. Our saved loved ones are being taken care of by the Caretaker of all caretakers. They are experiencing comfort, which is greater than any comfort on Earth. Their happiness reaches such a magnitude that we cannot even imagine. It is a lot easier to be happy in Heaven than to be happy on Earth.

Born-Again Christians have something spectacular to look forward to. If we should be grieving for anyone, we should be grieving for ourselves, who are still on Earth with all the trouble in the world. Our Christian deceased loved ones have it so much better than we do. With God's help, we will see God, Jesus, and our family of Born-Again believers. However, we do not have to wait until we reach Heaven to have peace. God gives us the opportunity to have peace while we are still living on earth. The Bible says in **Isaiah 26:3**, *"You will keep in perfect peace all who trust in You, whose thoughts are fixed on you."*

The body is a capsule for the soul. The body of a deceased

Christian is the least important part of that person. The most important part is the soul in Heaven with God. It is difficult not to be sad when you see the body of a deceased loved one, but we should concentrate on the soul. Knowing that the soul is with God should put us at peace.

We should not live in fear of our own death or the death of our loved ones. We should live each day enjoying our loved ones who are alive and enjoying our own lives.

Death in and of itself is not the worst thing that can happen to someone. The worst that can occur to someone is to die and not be Born-Again and miss out on eternal life.

Whether a saved believer wakes up on Earth or in Heaven, God is taking care of them.

## MY TESTIMONY: POSITIVE THOUGHTS AND AFFIRMATIONS

# Everything Will Be Okay

For a saved Christian, leaving the body is like leaving a shell so that the soul can make a journey to a better world.

What about if you do not know if your deceased loved one was Born-Again? Feel free to pray for them. Prayer can only help. It can never hurt. While they were on earth, they could have accepted Jesus and become Born-Again, and you do not know it. God knows their heart, and He loves them and wants them to be saved even more than we do. He is a loving, kind Father who wants everyone to be saved.

If there was any way to save your deceased loved ones, you can be sure that God did it. Try your best not to worry. Pray and ask God to give you peace and help you enjoy the rest of your life. You do not have control over that deceased loved one, but you could possibly have a significant impact on your loved ones who are still alive. You may be the one to tell them about Jesus and how to be saved. Ask God to assist you in telling them about the Gospel. Gently tell them and let them make a choice. Pray that God will save them and ask Him to help you accept and be at peace with whatever choice your loved one makes. Never give up on them becoming saved. However, we also have to be sure that we are saved. (Steps to salvation are given at the end of this book).

# A Big Part of Life Is Coping with Death

Practically everyone wants to go to Heaven, but almost no one wants to die. The problem is that you have to die and be Born-Again (by believing in and accepting Jesus Christ as your personal Savior) before you can go to Heaven. The Bible says in **John 3:16** "For God so loved the world that He gave His one and only Son, that whoever believes in Him shall not perish but have eternal life." It is worth it to be saved and Born-Again because **1 Corinthian 2:9** says, *"Eye has not seen, nor ear heard, nor have entered into the heart of man the things which God has prepared for those who love Him."* If only we could be like Enoch or Elijah, whom God took to Heaven without dying. To my knowledge, God never did it before and has not done it since. Therefore, we must face the fact that we cannot escape death. However, it is comforting to know that we will not die alone because God is always with us. We should pray for faith to keep trusting Him.

Of course, we want our loved ones to still be with us. We still wish they were on Earth and could enjoy a wonderful life. However, with God's help, we must accept that God took them. We must find peace with that fact. God loves and cares better for our loved ones than we ever could. Even our highest love for them could never measure up to the great magnitude of God's love for them.

## MY TESTIMONY: POSITIVE THOUGHTS AND AFFIRMATIONS

The following pages tell the steps needed to become Born Again for yourself or to lead others in the process. Also included are comforting Bible verses.

*If you disagree with these pages, please return it to whoever gave it to you. You may read the following page, know it already, and not need it. Please consider keeping it so you can copy it and give it to others who may need it (like your family, friends, and Church members). Thanks. Kindly copy this page and give it with the following page. You can copy it collated and stapled at a copy place.*

This is for everyone who wants their prayers to be answered by God. **Psalm 34:17** and **Proverbs 29:1-5** say that "The Lord hears the prayers of the righteous and delivers them out of all their troubles."

The righteous are those who are Born-Again and have given up their sins. If you need to become righteous and Born Again, please say this prayer.

*Dear Lord, Please make me Born Again. I am now accepting Jesus as my personal Savior and I believe that He died for all of my sins. Please save me and help me to believe that I am saved and please help me to give up my sins. In Jesus' name. Amen.*

*If you believe this, you are saved. Read* **Romans 10:9**. *Now you can pray and know that God hears your prayers and will answer them. You may not always get exactly what you ask for, but you can be sure that God will work things out because "All things work together for the good of those who love the Lord, to those who are called according to His purpose." (Romans 8:28).*

# Bible Verses

Give all your worries and cares to God, for He cares about what happens to you. (1 Peter 5:7)

You will keep in perfect peace all who trust in you, whose thoughts are fixed on you. (Isaiah 26:3)

I am leaving you with a gift-peace of mind and heart. And the peace I give isn't like the peace the world gives. So don't be troubled or afraid. (John 14:27)

Trust in Me in your times of trouble and I will rescue you and you will give me glory. (Psalm 50:15)

When I pray, You answer me. You encourage me by giving me the strength I need. (Psalm 138:3)

I can do everything with the help of Christ who gives me the strength I need. (Philippians 4:13)

The Lord gives His people strength. The Lord blesses them with peace. (Psalm 29:11)

Don't worry about anything: instead pray about everything. Tell God what you need and thank Him for all He has done. If you do this, you will experience God's peace which is far more wonderful than the human mind can understand. His peace will guard your hearts and minds as you live in Christ Jesus. (Phillipians 4:6),

My power works best in your weakness. (2 Corinthians 2:9)

God is our refuge and strength, always ready to help in times of trouble. So we'll not fear, even if the earthquakes come and the mountains crumble into the sea. (Psalm 46: 1-2)

People who do what is right may have many problems, but the

Lord will solve them all. (Psalm 34:19)

www.ingramcontent.com/pod-product-compliance
Lightning Source LLC
Chambersburg PA
CBHW041152110526
44590CB00027B/4211